CAPE POETRY PAPERBACKS

ROGER McGOUGH
AFTER THE MERRYMAKING

Roger McGough

AFTER THE MERRYMAKING

JONATHAN CAPE
THIRTY BEDFORD SQUARE LONDON

FIRST PUBLISHED 1971
REPRINTED 1973 (twice), 1975
© 1971 BY ROGER MCGOUGH

JONATHAN CAPE LTD
30 BEDFORD SQUARE, LONDON WC1

ISBN 0 224 00979 6

Some of these poems first appeared in: *Capella*, *Workshop 10*, *Second Aeon*, *The Sunday Times* and *Poetry Review*.

'Tranquillity' is reproduced by permission of the *Evening Standard*.

Printed in Great Britain by
Fletcher & Son Ltd, Norwich
and bound by
Richard Clay (The Chaucer Press) Ltd, Bungay, Suffolk

CONTENTS

III   THE AMAZING ADVENTURES OF P.C. PLOD

I AFTER THE MERRYMAKING

a cat, a horse and the sun

a cat mistrusts the sun
keeps out of its way
only where sun and shadow meet
it moves

a horse loves the sun
it basks all day
snorts
and beats its hooves

the sun likes horses
but hates cats
that is why it makes hay
and heats tin roofs

The sun no longer loves me

The sun no longer loves me.
When i sit waiting for her
in my little room
she arrives
not cheerfully
but out of a sense of duty
like a National Health prostitute.

Sometimes
she leans silky
against the wall
lolling and stretchy
but mostdays she fidgets
and scratches at clouds.
Whenever i ask her to stay the night
she takes umbrage
and is gone.

On having no one to write
a love poem about

thismorning
while strolling through my head
rummaging in litterbins
i found by the roadside
an image
that someone had thrown away
A rose

i picked it up
hurried into a backstreet
away from the busy thoroughfare of thoughts
and waited to give it
to the first girl who smiled at me

it's getting dark
and i'm still waiting
The rose attracts a fly

   getting dark
two groupies and a dumb broad
have been the only passersby

        dark
i chance a prayer
There is a smell of tinsel in the air.

after the merrymaking, love?

after the merrymaking,
love.
Back to my place
it's not far
a little shedevil
whoever you are.
It was great fun while I lasted.

after the love,
sleep.
In the onrush of its lava
we are caught
side by side
arms entangled
carcass to carcass.

after the sleep,
emptiness.
The sweat dry
and a little nearer death
we awake to meet the day
we say goodmorning
and I wish you five hundred miles away.

and the field screamed 'TRACTOR'

harvesttime
the sky
the inside of a giant balloon
sky blue
someone's yellow finger sticking through

late birds screech
wormless

waiting to be threshed
within an inch of its life
the field trembles

the pain
ohthepainoh
the pain

Train Crash

i once met a man
who had been in a crash
during the war

he said the worst thing
was the pause after
and the pause before

the bloody screaming
which though nervesplintttering
might well be heard

most nights on TV.
He spoke slowly
pausing between each word

Head Injury

I do not smile because I am happy.
Because I gurgle I am not content.
I feel in colours, mottled, mainly black.
And the only sound I hear is the sea
Pounding against the white cliffs of my skull.

For seven months I lay in a coma.
Agony.
Darkness.
My screams drowned by the wind
Of my imperceptible breathing.

One morning the wind died down. I awoke.

You are with me now as you are everyday
Seeking some glimmer of recognition
Some sign of recovery. You take my hand.
I try to say: 'I love you.'
Instead I squawk,
Eyes bobbing like dead birds in a watertank.
I try to say: 'Have pity on me, pity on yourself
Put a bullet between the birds.'
Instead I gurgle.
You kiss me then walk out of the room.
I see your back.
I feel a colour coming, mottled, mainly black.

There are fascists

there are
fascists
pretending
to be
humanitarians

like
cannibals
on a health kick
eating only
vegetarians

Uncle Harry

Uncle Harry was a widower
wouldn't have it anyother way
wore two pair of socks all year round
with a prayer started each day:

> 'Oh God, let it be a coronary
> something quick and clean
> I've always been fastidious
> and death can be obscene.
> So if today You've put me down
> then it's Your will and I'm not scared
> but could it be at home please
> not where I'll look absurd,
> like on the street, at the match,
> in the toilet on a train
> (and preferably a one off
> in the heart and not the brain)'

Uncle Harry was a vegetarian
until the other day
collapsed on his way to the Health Food Store,
rushed to hospital, died on the way.

Dunenudes

a pinta makes a man
thats so very true
i know cos i'm a milkman
and my friend is too

a pinta shapes a girl
thats so very true
we found her on a sanddune
the sky a poster blue

milk will soon turn sour
thats so very true
so we lay among the pintas
without anymore ado

the bottles now are broken
the milk has slaked the sand
and we walk into the sunset
hand in hand in hand

dreampoem

I forsake dusty springfield
to follow you out of the theatre.
You are friendly but not affectionate.
I haven't seen you for ages.
You now have a son.
I overhear you telling a stranger
that he is called Menelaus
after the son of my mistress.

I follow you through vast antique shops
where I consider buying a throne.
Instead I go out into the busy road
and under a flyover.
You are nowhere in sight.
The searchlight in the citycentre
is still fingering the sky
though it is now well after midday.

Realizing that I will never see you again
and overwhelmed with whatmighthavebeenness
I give myself up
at the nearest marriage bureau.

All is not well with the child murderers

in the security wing
all is not well
with the childmurderers
first
the cocoastrike scare
then soap sharpening and
pillowfights on the stair
close scrutiny reveals
mutiny in the air

they have been warned
the governor is adamant
anymore of this and they'll be thrown
to the public

Flying

from the ground
one sees only the arse end of clouds
those bits of the blanket
tucked under

Flying
one sees across the counterpane
rumpled, morning white,
as if the earth had spent
another restless night

Tranquillity

Tranquillity
two deep space divers
walk about
on the bottom of the Sea

in a junglestream
two lovers bathe
laugh and throw tigerlilies
at the peeping tom moon

on a hillside
two shepherds watch
'If there's a God,' said one,
'why isn't there life up there?'

the ship
laden with moonmariners
and buried treasure blasts off
Tranquillity

Sunday before Xmas

```
RAIN   a dog        RAIN
RAIN   runs the     RAIN
RAIN   gauntlet     RAIN
RAIN   of drip      RAIN
RAIN   ping trees   RAIN
```

at home
plainclothes santas
sniffle and snooze
between opening hours
dreaming of grottoes
stacked with woodnymphs
and fairies
hot and plump
as chestnuts

```
DRIZZLEDISMAL
DRIZZZEDISMAL
DRIZZZZDISMAL
DRIZZZZZISMAL
DRIZZZZZZSMAL
DRIZZZZZZZMAL
```

mistaking it for the 'Big 'ouse' and bold as braces
a skinhead revolves into the Adelphi.
Before the porters can move
the residents are upon him.
Aldermen, Executives and Young Liberals
boot him around the foyer
    'heelchapsheel'

Rotarians and Freemasons all muck in together
blood skids off patent leather
    'onononononon'
until like a red and white rattle
he lies splintered on the marble.
The toffs adjust their dickies
'Shall we join the ladies?'

The morningafter
the night of the officeparty
locked in an empty building
a lone typist
naked, except for a seethru blouse
and a paper hat
covers herself with balloons and mistletoe
goes to the window
and waves frantically for help.
A passerby smiles and waves back.

The sky is the colour of old saucepans.

Ex art student

Neat-haired and
low-heeled
you live without passion

hold down
a dull job
in the world of low fashion

ambition
once prickly
is limpid is static

portfolioed
your dreams
lie now in the attic

Bucket

everyevening after tea
grandad would take his bucket for a walk

An empty bucket

When i asked him why
he said because it was easier to carry

grandad had
an answer
for everything

Railings

towards the end of his tether
grandad
at the drop of a hat
would paint the railings

overnight
we became famous
allover the neighbourhood
for our smart railings

(and our dirty hats)

dawnmare on 24th St

talking
like we'd known eachother for years.
One hand on your heart
the other on my guitar
you pledge your troth.
A prostitute
takes a swing at someguy
with a ketchup bottle.
No one takes much notice
least of all the guy.

4 a.m. already.
Known eachother less than an hour
when I stumbled into the last ounce
of Paul Colby's party
(one of those Village Frontier scenes,
bagels, bangles and beans).
Someenchantedevening
acrossacrowdedroom etc
I can't believe my luck.

Then you tell me you need heroin
and could I let you have seven dollars.
Together we go to the counter
and I pay 50 cents for the coffee.
As we leave, the prostitute screams
and reaches for the ketchup.
It's getting light.
I give you four dollars, all I have.
You kiss goodbye, no reason now to stay
i walk to my hotel, a poem's throw away.

You may get the vote at eighteen, but you're born with a price on your head

blue sierra
daguerreoscape
echo   echo
in some moonfilled canyon
as a rattlesnake
tosses in its sleep

Time to move on
I kick out the fire
and to the ground put my ear

He's still there
getting nearer year by year.
The Bountyhunter
who knows my price
closing in.
White bones gleaming like dice
high heel boots
dusty
as sin

Gift for a lonely girl

Here's a poem for you love
Put it under your pillow
and who knows tonight
when you've cast your clothes
to the four corners of your dreams
Singers tall as trees
with velvet thighs
and eyes that tease
will assemble, and in sweetest tone
sing songs composed for you alone

And the one with eyes
the skiest blue, will take you,
take you walking through
fields as yet unknown to you
And the beauty that you keep inside
your soul, will moisten, open wide
for love's a flower you've cultivated
with tears, these years you've dreamed and waited

And so tonight
As you walk kneedeep in stars
brighter than the brightest ones
I wish you this:
May tomorrow you find love
And have many sons

Storm

They're at it again
the wind and the rain
It all started
when the wind
took the window
by the collar
and shook it
with all its might
Then the rain
butted in
What a din
they'll be at it all night
Serves them right
if they go home in the morning
and the sky won't let them in

middle

couple

ten

when

game

and

go

the

will

be

tween

Love

aged

playing

nis

the

ends

they

home

net

still

be

them

The newly pressed suit

Here is a poem for the two of us to play.
Choose any part from the following:
> The *hero*
> The *heroine*
> The *bed*
> The *bedroom*
> The *newly pressed suit*
(I will play the VILLAIN)

The poem begins late this evening
>   at a poetryreading
Where the *hero* and the *heroine*
Are sitting and drinking and thinking
>   of making love.
At 10.30 they leave the pub and hurryhome
Once inside the flat they waste no time.
The hero quickly undresses the *heroine*,
carries her naked into the *bedroom*
and places her gently upon the *bed*
like a *newly pressed suit.*

Just then I step into the poem.
With a sharp left hook
I render unconscious the *hero*
And with a cruel laugh
Rape the *heroine*
(The raping continues for several stanzas)

>   Thank you for playing.

When you go out tonight
I hope you have better luck in your poem
Than you had in mine.

Pantomime poem

'HE'S BEHIND YER!'
chorused the children
but the warning came too late.

The monster leaped forward
and fastening its teeth into his neck,
tore off the head.

The body fell to the floor
'MORE' cried the children
'MORE, MORE, MORE

MORE

II LOVE POEMS
FROM THE '69–'71 WAR

Bulletins

We sit in front of the wireless
waiting for the latest news
on the state of our affair
You knitting socks for our footballers overseas
me wishing i was there
The bulletins are more frequent now
they are broadcast by the hour
The headline in the *Echo* reads
'Love turned Sour'

McGough's last stand

FIRST REEL

it can't just end like this
no one to witness my plight
no sense of history
not a photographer in sight

broken promises lie thick on the ground
and i'm down to my last keg of nostalgia

tears running down your warpaint
you close in
screaming:
'white man make love with forked tongue!'

Hurrah! here comes the cavalry

END OF FIRST REEL

SECOND REEL

Oh no!
it's a platoon of exlovers
led by your first husband
(saturday morning matinees were never like this)
it's all over
the Battle of Shit Creek

At sundown
on an upturned wagon
a lone bugler plays the Last Post
i ask you for a dance
you give me a belt
to my scalp

THE END

Vandal

at first
we had a landscape to ourselves
Then the vandals moved in

deflowered the verges
put the carp before the horse
                        and worse
chopped down our initialled trees
bonfired the bench
on which we'd had our first kiss
threw stones
and chased you away

This morning
one of them was caught
He turned out to be me
I am due to appear in court next week
Charged
with emotion

Trenchwarfare

after the battle of the Incriminating Loveletter
there came an uneasy truce
We still sleep together in the same trench
but you have built
a wall of sandbags in between

somenights
gutsy and fullofight
rifle in hand
I'm over the top
brave asa ram

and you're always waiting,
my naked sentry
'Halt, who goes there? Friend or lover?'
'Lover'
'Advance lover'

in the morning
whistling 'itsalongwaytotipperary'
i trudge across the skyline
to the office

Buddies

for the Angies'
with one
small alteration!

We were drafted into the same unit
and shipped out to the front
Shared the same lousy rations
became buddies all through the war
Two guns are better than one
that's what buddies are for

We fought the enemy side by side
and occasionally fought eachother
When they gave us hell
we gave them more
Cried after the first battle
that's what buddies are for

Then peace broke out
and we sailed into the orangeblossom sunset
Wondered how long it would last
once we were safe ashore
Now you tell me were are having our first babys
that's what buddies are for

Amateur traumatics

When you starred in *my* play
you were just right.
I gave you rave notices
night after night.

But you wanted bigger and better parts.
Upstarts
sent you script after script.
You counted your lines
then you flipped. You just flipped.

Hash Wednesday

last wednesday
it all clicked

you only wanted me for my loveandaffection
my generosity
and my undyingfaithfulness

(to you my prizegiven rosaries meant nothing,
my holy relics, merely relics)

Begone oh Belial's daughter
I wash my hands of you in holy water

next year i will live alone
and breed racehorses
in the attic

The Mongrel

When i came to live with you
i brought a brighteyed pup
and as our love matured
so the pup grew up

you fed him and you trained him
asif he were your own
you pampered him looked after him
until he was full grown

then you went away
        now he's uncontrollable
                inconsolable

mistresses they come and go
look pretty much the same
they pat his head and stroke his back
and say they're glad they came

but he's no longer interested
in feminine acclaim
and when they try new tricks
he tires quickly of the game

he skulks around the kitchen
looking old and slightly lame
at night he howls at the window
asif the moon's to blame

and with every sad encounter
i realize to my shame
that my sadeyed mongrel
answers only to your name.

P.O.W.

it wouldn't be wise to go away together
not even for a weekend.
A few bouts of neocopulation
in a Trust House in the Midlands
would not be the answer.

I commit my sins gentle
Prefer my adultery mental.

Though we feel the need to escape
sometimes
The need for a scape-
goat sometimes
You my muddled tunnel
I your Wooden Horse
We'd only keep running all night
then give ourselves up at first light.

You see I don't love you
And though you're as beautiful as she was
it wouldn't be wise to go away together.
My sense of duty would trouble you
I'm a semi-detached P.O.W.

Three weeks ago we decided to go our separate ways

Three weeks ago we decided to go our separate ways
not overnight, but whenever was convenient.

There is a fragility now
about our lovemaking
asif each time might be the last
The finger tends to linger
where once it hurried past.

And as the end of our relationship looms
the excitement of the start it assumes.
There are new awakenings
erotic as in a dream
With each sacrificial offering
the more virginal we seem
Old scars become new wounds
when kissed overmuch
And memories longhardened
now moisten to the touch.

Love is a circle
we've completed the course
Now we savour the honeymoon
before the divorce.

And with all we've discovered together
And with all the experience gained
that final
mad
sad
fuck
will achieve the perfection
that only the first attained
That final
mad
sad

i wanted one life
you wanted another
we couldn't have our cake
so we ate eachother.

III   THE AMAZING ADVENTURES OF P.C. PLOD

P.C. Plod at the pillar box

It's snowing out
streets are thiefproof
a wind that blows
straight up yer nose
no messin
A night
not fit to be seen with a dog
out in

On the corner
P.C. Plod (brave as a mountain lion)
carefully affixes a 5d stamp
on a letter
before posting it to his cousin
in South Africa
In March he plans
to emigrate
Springbox or no Springbox

P.C. Plod versus
the Dale St Dog strangler

For several months
Liverpool was held in the grip of fear
by a dogstrangler most devilish,
who roamed the streets after dark
looking for strays. Finding one
he would tickle it seductively
about the body to gain its confidence,
then lead it down a deserted backstreet
where he would strangle the poor brute.
Hardly a night passed without somebody's
faithful fourlegged friend being dispatched
to that Golden Kennel in the sky.

The public were warned,
At the very first sign
of anything suspicious,
ring Canine-nine-nine.

Nine o'clock on the evening of January 11th sees P.C. Plod
on the corner of Dale St and Sir Thomas St
disguised as a Welsh collie.
It is part of a daring plan to apprehend the strangler.
For though it is a wet and moonless night,
Plod is cheered in the knowledge
that the whole of the Liverpool City Constabulary
is on the beat that night disguised as dogs.
Not ten minutes earlier, a pekinese (Policewoman Hodges)
had scampered past on her way to Clayton Square.

For Plod, the night passed uneventfully
and so in the morning he was horrified to learn
that no less than fourteen policemen and policewomen
had been tickled and strangled during the night.

The public were horrified
The Commissioner aghast
Something had to be done
And fast.

P.C. Plod (wise as a brace of owls)
met the challenge magnificently
and submitted an idea so startling in its vision
so audacious in its conception
that the Commissioner gasped
before ordering all dogs in the city
to be thereinafter disguised as fuzz.
The plan worked
and the dogstrangler was heard of no more.

Cops and mongrels
like P.C.s in a pod
To a grateful public
Plod was God.

So next time you're up in Liverpool
take a closer look at that
policeman on pointduty, he might
well be a cocker spaniel.

P.C. Plod versus the Park Road Rapist

'Hello, Hello, Hello'
thought P.C. Plod
(cunning as a pack of foxes)
'the man sitting opposite me
here in this typical cosy cafe
is identikal to the identikit
picture of the Park Road Rapist.'

Plod mentioned the coincidence
and they both agreed
the resemblance was uncanny
So over a pot of tea
they discussed the case
crime in general
and Everton's chances of winning the Cup.

Eventually
the man looked at his watch
thanked the kindly copper for the tea
and leaving the typical cosy cafe
headed for Park Road.

Noodle bug

One bright Thursday morning
P.C. Plod was on pointduty in Williamson Square
when he was approached by an oriental gentleman,
new to the city, who wanted to know
the whereabouts of a certain Chinese restaurant.
To Plod, one Chinese restaurant was as good,
or as bad, as another, and so he
directed the old man to the nearest.

Ten minutes later, the old man returned:
'Please could you dilect me to Yuet Ben Lestaurant'
'That's a coincidence' remarked Plod
'You're the second Chinaman to ask me that in ten minutes,
is there a party on?'
'Me same Chinaman,' explained the same Chinaman.
To cover up his embarrassment,
Plod gave detailed directions
of a restaurant on the far side of the city.
The old man trundled off.

Twenty minutes later, tired and angry,
he was back in Williamson Square.
Lest a member of our Police Force be thought
less than wonderful and idiotic to boot,
Plod sought immediately to pacify
the stranger with polite conversation.
'Now then sir what have you there in that large bag
that weighs so heavily upon you?'
'In bag there is special Chinese flour'
'And what's that used for sir?'
persisted the trafficontrolling seeker
of eternal truth and wisdom.

D

'Ah well, special flour is mixed with water until
velly soft and then whole family arrive for
ceremony and everybody pull and roll and pull
and roll and pull and roll until we have big soft
noodle six foot in length'
'Garn, silliest thing I ever heard' scoffed Plod
'What could you do with a big soft noodle six foot long?'
'You could put it on pointduty in Williamson Square'
suggested the old man and

                        ran

                                off

                                        down

                                                the

                                                        page

Nasty business

'RAPE' screamed the girl 'RAPE'

'Not while I'm on duty thank you,'
replied P.C. Plod politely but firmly.

'No I mean I've been raped'
hystericked the girl.

'Ah, then that would explain
why your clothes are disarranged
and your hair awry.'

'Just so,' concluded the girl
and fell to the pavement
like a body.

'Cup of tea'd go down a treat,'
thought P.G. Plod
and turned down Hardman Street.
'Nasty business, Rape (sniff)
Nasty business.'

The Sergeant gets a handsome deal

'Quiet tonight'
suggested Sergeant Lerge
seeing P.C. Plod in Boot's doorway.
'As a truncheon'
was Plod's reply (rich in simile).
'Anything at all?'
'Pair of drunks and a drug peddler Sarge.'
'Drug peddler eh. I trust you
apprehended the villain?'
'Indeed Sarge'
'What was his cargo?'
'Marijuana'
'What kind?'
'Congo red.'
'How much?'
'Four quid an ounce'
'Reasonable. I'll take a half'
'To you, thirty bob'
'That's a handsome deal Constable'
'You're a handsome sergeant, Sergeant.'

P.C. Plod versus Maggie May

P.C. Plod was cruising up and down old Canning Place
dreaming of a better life for all of us
when he spied a figure famous in those parts
'twas Maggie May, the uncrowned Queen of Tarts.
Plod quickly removed his boots
and followed her on tiptoe.
When eventually she took up her position
(one of many) beside a lamppost
he ducked behind a parking meter
to observe the High Priestess of Venereal Therapy
ply her immoral trade.
From his advantage point, Plod
(stealthy as an iguana) made extensive notes
on the comings and goings of his quarry
and of the men with whom she contorted.
They ranged from sailors to surgeons
from fishmongers to fieldmarshals
'The sins of the flesh' observed Plod,
'are not the divine right of the poor.'
All night Plod crouched and waited
until he had collected enough evidence
to put Maggie behind bars for thirty years
(or alternatively a fine of forty shillings).
And as the sun clocked in for the early shift
and seagulls on ferries were hitching a lift
he knew it was time to spring into action.
He stood up, only to find
that at some point during his lonely vigil
a sneakthief had made off with his boots.
But there was no time for Plod to ponder
on the depths to which tealeaves will sink
for Maggie May had spotted him
and was already halfway down Paradise Street.
Like a two-footed gazelle

Plod fullpelted after her in his bobby sox
Soon he was abreast of her
'I abreast you in the name of the law'
he panted 'and anything you say
will be taken down and may be used
in evidence against you.'
'Knickers' said Maggie.
They stopped, and true to his word
Plod knelt and removed the flimsy evidence.
And as workers whistled on factory floors
and the seamen's dispensary opened its doors
through the morning rushhour he led away
that dirty rotten lowdown (though some say
with a heart of gold) Maggie May.

P.C. Plod in Love

Sergeant Lerge put down his knife and fork
and turning to Plod, said
'Yummyyumyummy, yummyyummy yum yum'
and began to lick his lips.
'Stop licking my lips' said Plod
and moved further down the table.
The Sergeant apologized.
'I'm sorry constable, ... forgot myself for the minute
a bad habit I got into at the Police College'
and muttering something
about the way the light from the canteen window
brought a magical softness to Plod's cheeks
he stood up and flustered his way out.
Plod, his appetite gone,
pushed away the remains of his sultana pud
and went into a brown study.
Five minutes later there was a knock
on the study door.
'Come' said Plod.
In came the lovely Policewoman Hodges.
'Sorry to disturb you Constable,
but I believe I left my handbag
on the chair behind you.'
Plod stood to let her pass
and as she did
he felt her serge with pleasure.
This was his opportunity
The moment he'd been waiting
for
for
ages ' ... er I was wondering ... er ... if ... er ...
I have a spare ticket for the policeman's ball
next Saturday ... and ... er ... I ...'
he stumbled over the words.

W.P.C. Hodges helped him gently to his feet.
'I'd love to come with you' she purred
'I'll meet you in O'Connors Tavern at 20.00 hours.'
Plod watched her disappear through the doorway
and feeling that no one man
deserved such happiness
and unable to contain the emotion
made his way downstairs to the bridewell
where, in the loneliness of an empty cell
wept, till the tears ran down his tunic.

P.C. Plod's adventures in the skin trade

♩Maybe it's because I'm not a Londoner♩
whistled Plod, hicking his way
through the crowded streets of the capital,
♩that I love London so.♩
He had just completed a two-day refresher course
in studentbaiting at Scotland Yard
and having a few hours left
before catching his train to Liverpool
the refreshed bobby was happy
to sightsee and windowgaze.
Suddenly he sightsaw a supermarket.
'Just the ticket' he thought
'Shops'll be shut when I get home
so a tin of beans bought now
will guarantee a nourishing and tasty supper.'
He went in.

P.C. Plod (shrewd as a pelican)
soon realized that this was no ordinary supermarket
but one of the sexual variety
whose weekly adverts in the *Police Gazette*
had both amazed and troubled him.
The shop was jampacked with latenight shoppers.
There was no turning back.
Like virginal flotsam on a sea of Eros worshippers
Plod was carried, eyes closed, past the rows
of aphrodisiacs creams and condoms.
Carnalcopia, the devil's Repository.

Any hopes that Plod fondly held
in his banging blue breast,
of being washed safely ashore
on the pavement outside
were dashed, when he realized

that the exit was guarded
by a lady armed with a cash register,
and he, wet and empty handed.
If there was one thing Plod hated more
than unbridled filth, it was making a scene.
He looked around wildly for some innocent memento,
some harmless souvenir. His prayers were answered.
'Aha, I'll get one of these inhalers
and give it to Sergeant Lerge.'
So saying he selected a Swedish vibrator
and carried it proudly to the cash desk.
'Just what I was looking for'
he explained cheerfully. 'Of course it's not for me
it's for the Sergeant, sinus trouble.'
'Takes all sorts' thought the young lady
as Plod scuttled down Edgware Road
beanless.

P.C. Plod versus
the Youth International Party

P.C. Plod had just come off pointduty
in Yates Wine Lodge
and was making his way back to the cop shop
for a meat pie and a liedown
when he suddenly realized
that he was lost.
As was his custom in cases like this
he looked for a member of the public
to assist him.
For purposes of this poem, the one
nearest to hand was a Yippie.
'I'm sorry to trouble you sir, but could
you direct me to the nearest police station?'
'Pig' said the Yippie
'Pig.'
Plod smiled. 'Perhaps I have not made
myself quite clear ... ' he began.
The Yippie produced a water pistol from
his handbag and directed a stream
into Plod's good eye.
'Pig' said the Yippie
'Pig. Pig.'
''pon my soul' muttered the peeved P.C.
and moving with the speed of a man
twice his size drew from beneath his
policecape a sawnoff potato shotgun.
The Yippie blanched.
'Pig' he hissed.
'Badger' retorted Plod
and with deadly aim let go four and
a half rounds of King Edwards.
The youngman fell in a heap.

'Silly place to leave a heap'
thought BonnyandPlod and bareheaded
for the nearest barrowlady
to refill his helmet
with ammo.

Goodbye P.C. Plod

P.C. Plod was sitting in St Johns Gardens
feeding the stoolpigeons
and writing a fan letter to Hercule Poirot
when a message came through
that His Holiness the Chief Constable
wished to see him.
The Chief Constable himself!
Was this to be promotion at last?
Would he be admitted to the plainclothesed elite
Get the chance, like his heart, to skip the beat?
As there was no time to waste
he set off, post haste, for H.Q.

Plod jogged all the way
through the bustling city streets
(pausing only once
to help an aged shoplifter across the road).
And passersby applauded
this Guardian Angel of the law
and as he jogged he daydreamed
of the glories lying in store.

One

Two

Three

Four

Five minutes later Plod panted to a halt
outside the Chief's office.
He mopped his brow, then his boots,
knocked and entered.
'P.C. Plod reporting as requested sir'
The Chief Constable closed his autographed
copy of *Mein Kampf* and looked up

'Now look here constable   ... ... etc.
Good man and all that ... ... etc.
Rumours going round division... ... ... etc.
Appearing in poems of dubious nature ... ... etc.
Unprofessional conduct ... ... etc.
Bad for image ... ... etc.
Three months' suspension as from now ... ... etc.
You may go   ... ... etc.'

'But sir I know nothing about this'
protested Plod, 'true as I'm standing here.'
'No back answers Constable' cantankered the Chief.
'You may go'

Plod reeled out of the office
and flabbergasted down the corridor.
It was all too painful.
Like a man in a dream
he made his way to the lockerroom
where he hung up his truncheon
and changed into the old tweed jacket
he always wore off duty.
He paused for what seemed like a moment,
then took down the photographs
of W.P.C. Hodges, Dinah Rigg and Sir Robert Peel
that were Sellotaped to the inside of the door.
Without a word to anybody he left H.Q.
to begin his cruel sentence.
It was all too painful.

Eyes downcast he walked along Hope St
his mind wracked
with the torment of innocence ...
'Good afternoon P.C. Plod'
chorused a giggle of schoolgirls
waiting at the busstop.
Plod returned the greeting
then bravely brushed away a tear.
And he continued his lonely journey
until he reached the Cathedral
where he went in to seek comfort
and to say a prayer for us all,
everyone.